# MUSTARD SEED
### *Pocket*
# PRAYERS
### *Of*
# RENEWAL

## M. J. Welcome

## Other Books by M. J. Welcome

Spiritual Diseases of the Unbridled Tongue

Understanding the Power of God's Word

The 21-Day Crucifixion Challenge

Overcome Secret Sins in 15 Days

Seeking Total Restoration

Battling for the Light

Copyright © 2016 Michelle J. Dyett-Welcome.

All rights reserved. No Part of this book may be reproduced, stored in retrieval system, or transmitted by any means without the written permission of the author.

SMART PUBLISHING HOUSE
A Division of MDW Consulting Group
Far Rockaway, New York
www.smartpublishinghouse.com

Editing | Layout S.M.A.R.T Copy Designs
Proofreaders | Mary Ball | Matteel Welcome
S.M.A.R.T Copy Designs
www.smartcopydesignsinc.com

First Published by Smart Publishing House 09/28/16

Library of Congress Control Number: 2016916277

ISBN-10:0-9978268-2-7
ISBN-13:978-0-9978268-2-1

Scripture quotations are from the Holy Bible, King James Version unless otherwise specified. Hebrew and Greek meanings from Strong's Concordance.

Printed in the U.S.A

# Table of Contents

Appreciation ................................................. vii

Introduction ................................................. ix

Day 1 ........................................................... 13

   Deliverance ............................................. 13

Day 2 ........................................................... 15

   Manifestation ........................................... 15

Day 3 ........................................................... 16

   Live ........................................................... 17

Day 4 ........................................................... 19

   Freedom .................................................. 19

Day 5 ........................................................... 21

   Educate ................................................... 21

Day 6 ........................................................... 22

   Fill ............................................................ 23

Day 7 ........................................................... 25

   Break ....................................................... 25

Day 8 ........................................................... 27

   Forgive .................................................... 27

Day 9 ........................................................... 29

   Work ........................................................ 29

| | |
|---|---|
| Day 10 | 30 |
| Gifts | 31 |
| Day 11 | 32 |
| Clean | 33 |
| Day 12 | 34 |
| Stagnancy | 35 |
| Day 13 | 36 |
| Nourish | 37 |
| Day 14 | 39 |
| Quench | 39 |
| Day 15 | 41 |
| Uproot | 41 |
| Day 16 | 43 |
| Removal | 43 |
| Day 17 | 45 |
| Preserve | 45 |
| Day 18 | 46 |
| Seal | 47 |
| Day 19 | 48 |
| Walk | 49 |
| Day 20 | 51 |
| Overflow | 51 |

Day 21 .................................................................. 52
   Understanding ............................................ 53
Day 22 .................................................................. 54
   Newness ...................................................... 55
Day 23 .................................................................. 56
   Baptism ....................................................... 57
Day 24 .................................................................. 58
   Mouth .......................................................... 59
Day 25 .................................................................. 60
   Cleanse ........................................................ 61
Day 26 .................................................................. 62
   Cry ............................................................... 63
Day 27 .................................................................. 64
   Interference ................................................ 65
Day 28 .................................................................. 66
   Condemn .................................................... 67
Day 29 .................................................................. 69
   Proof ............................................................ 71
Day 30 .................................................................. 73
   Magnify ....................................................... 73
Conclusion .. **Error! Bookmark not defined.**

## Appreciation

Holy Spirit, I thank you for placing this project on my heart. I thank you for giving each days prayer and for the anointing, which rests upon it. May countless lives be changed as we link a strong prayer chain together in the spirit. Do what you have planned to do with them. May they be a sweet and savory odor before your throne of grace.

To my precious friend Mary thank you again for your help on this project! You are a blessing to the kingdom of God and to me.

To my son Matteel thank you for your willingness to help me proof each project with a pleasant attitude. May the Lord continue to bless you. Your service has honored me. It has blessed me and I desire the Lord to richly bless you.

To all the others who helped with this project thank you for your encouragement and participation in the online posting of the prayer starter series. Your prayers have been a blessing to me personally but also to the advancement of the kingdom. May God bless you richly for you saw it not robbery to invest your time to add your prayer link to the spiritual prayer chain daily.

# Introduction

God has called us to be members of his household. The Lord's house will be called a house of prayer according to Isaiah 56:7. Therefore, it is imperative that each of us learn how to flow in prayer. It is not with a multitude of words but in the quality and soundness of our prayers that will cause God to move on our behalf.

*"In the multitude of words there wanteth not sin: but he that refraineth his lips is wise." Proverbs 10:19*

*"The Pharisee stood and prayed thus with himself, God, I thank thee, that I am not as other men are, extortioners, unjust, adulterers, or even as this publican." Luke 18:11*

*"But when ye pray, use not vain repetitions, as the heathen do: for they think that they shall be heard for their much speaking." Matthew 6:7*

Vain repetitions does not ensure that God will hear us when we speak to him, but rather the sincerity of our hearts.

*"And the publican, standing afar off, would not lift up so much as his eyes unto heaven, but smote upon his breast, saying, God be merciful to me a sinner."* Luke 18:13

The prayer prompts in this book are designed to help believers to pray for themselves and for one another in one accord. To each prayer prompt add your prayer link. It can be a sentence or a paragraph. As you do, you will join others in creating a prayer chain that is spiritually strong and sound in the Lord. Through the power and work of Holy Spirit, we will be knitted together in the bond of love and in the spirit of agreement.

*"That their hearts might be comforted, being knit together in love, and unto all riches of the full assurance of understanding, to the acknowledgement of the mystery of God, and of the Father, and of Christ;"* Colossians 2:2

*"Again I say unto you, That if two of you shall agree on earth as touching any thing that they shall ask, it shall be done for them of my Father which is in heaven."* Matthew 18:19

One of the blessings we have through Christ Jesus is that we are not alone. Although we may be in different parts of the world, the Spirit of God unites us. Through our prayers, we will touch heaven and heaven will come down to touch us on the firm earth.

My prayer is that your prayer life will be revolutionized forever. May Holy Spirit move you to your next level by the power of the Spirit of Jesus. May our love for him and for one another secure territory for the kingdom.

*"But ye are not in the flesh, but in the Spirit, if so be that the Spirit of God dwell in you. Now if any man have not the Spirit of Christ, he is none of his."* Romans 8:9

Blessings!

M. J. Welcome

# Day 1

Deliverance

Father, in the name of Jesus deliver us from conflicting thoughts and tormenting doubts.

*"Casting down imaginations, and every high thing that exalteth itself against the knowledge of God, and bringing into captivity every thought to the obedience of Christ;" 2 Corinthians 10:5*

🔗 Meditate on the scripture with Holy Spirit then add your prayer link on the next page.

# Day 2

### Manifestation

Holy Spirit, I need you today please manifest in my life in a special way, amen.

*"That which is born of the flesh is flesh; and that which is born of the Spirit is spirit." John 3:6*

🕊 Meditate on the scripture with Holy Spirit then add your prayer link on the next page.

# Day 3

Live

Father, help me to live my life for you continually.

*"Yea, in the way of thy judgments, O Lord, have we waited for thee; the desire of our soul is to thy name, and to the remembrance of thee." Isaiah 26:8*

🕯 Meditate on the scripture with Holy Spirit then add your prayer link on the next page.

## Day 4

### Freedom

Father, help me to live a life free of delusion. Free of selfish ambitions. Free of a need to please and gain their approval. Help me to live a life free from the servitude to sin or to the enemy in the name of Jesus. Amen.

*"If the Son therefore shall make you free, ye shall be free indeed." John 8:36*

Meditate on the scripture with Holy Spirit then add your prayer link on the next page.

# Day 5

### Educate

Holy Spirit, educate me in the ways of the spirit. Teach me how to place humanistic (wisdom of man) and sensory (emotional or fleshly) learning under the Lordship of Jesus.

*"But the anointing which ye have received of him abideth in you, and ye need not that any man teach you: but as the same anointing teacheth you of all things, and is truth, and is no lie, and even as it hath taught you, ye shall abide in him." 1 John 2:27*

*"And they shall not teach every man his neighbour, and every man his brother, saying, Know the Lord: for all shall know me, from the least to the greatest." Hebrews 8:11*

🖋 Meditate on the scripture with Holy Spirit then add your prayer link on the next page.

# Day 6

## Fill

Father, I ask you to fill my soul with a deeper longing for you. I want to pant after you.

*"To the chief Musician, Maschil, for the sons of Korah. As the hart panteth after the water brooks, so panteth my soul after thee, O God" Psalm 42:1*

🌿 Meditate on the scripture with Holy Spirit then add your prayer link on the next page.

# Day 7

### Break

Father, break the tabernacle of flesh that hinders and opposes Holy Spirits work being made perfect in my life.

*"And they that are Christ's have crucified the flesh with the affections and lusts."*
*Galatians 5:24*

🔖 Meditate on the scripture with Holy Spirit then add your prayer link on the next page.

# Day 8

Forgive

Lord, forgive me for any lies that I have spoken to Holy Spirit known or unknown. Forgive me if I have tried to use the spirit of God for my own benefit.

*"But Peter said, Ananias, why hath Satan filled thine heart to lie to the Holy Ghost, and to keep back part of the price of the land? Whiles it remained, was it not thine own? and after it was sold, was it not in thine own power? why hast thou conceived this thing in thine heart? thou hast not lied unto men, but unto God." Acts 5:3-4*

🖋 Meditate on the scripture with Holy Spirit then add your prayer link on the next page.

# Day 9

### Work

Holy Spirit, identify the work that I am called to do. Set me on the right path in life, in Jesus name, amen.

*"As they ministered to the Lord, and fasted, the Holy Ghost said, Separate me Barnabas and Saul for the work whereunto I have called them." Acts 13:2*

🖋 Meditate on the scripture with Holy Spirit then add your prayer link on the next page.

# Day 10

### Gifts

Holy Spirit, identify the gifts of the spirit that has been given to me according to your will. Lord the manifestation of the Spirit is given to every man to profit withal. Cause me to be of benefit in the earth. Amen.

*"For to one is given by the Spirit the word of wisdom; to another the word of knowledge by the same Spirit; To another faith by the same Spirit; to another the gifts of healing by the same Spirit; To another the working of miracles; to another prophecy; to another discerning of spirits; to another divers kinds of tongues; to another the interpretation of tongues: But all these worketh that one and the selfsame Spirit, dividing to every man severally as he will."*
*1 Corinthians 12:8-11*

Meditate on the scripture with Holy Spirit then add your prayer link on the next page.

# Day 11

### Clean

Holy Spirit, help me to spiritually, physically, and emotionally clean my life today and keep it clean every day.

*"Whosoever is born of God doth not commit sin; for his seed remaineth in him: and he cannot sin, because he is born of God." 1 John 3:9*

 Meditate on the scripture with Holy Spirit then add your prayer link on the next page.

# Day 12

Stagnancy

Lord, remove stagnancy from around me. Make the atmosphere around me fresh and full of vitality. Restore abundant life unto me.

*"The thief cometh not, but for to steal, and to kill, and to destroy: I am come that they might have life, and that they might have it more abundantly." John 10:10*

🖋 Meditate on the scripture with Holy Spirit then add your prayer link on the next page.

# Day 13

### Nourish

Father, nourish me with your spirit. I do not want to starve. Lead me to the pasture of God.

*"And Jesus said unto them, I am the bread of life: he that cometh to me shall never hunger; and he that believeth on me shall never thirst." John 6:35*

🔖 Meditate on the scripture with Holy Spirit then add your prayer link on the next page.

## Day 14

### Quench

Father, quench my thirst by your Spirit. Never let me be dry. Never let me be thirsty.

*"Jesus answered and said unto her, Whosoever drinketh of this water shall thirst again: But whosoever drinketh of the water that I shall give him shall never thirst; but the water that I shall give him shall be in him a well of water springing up into everlasting life." John 4:13-14*

🔖 Meditate on the scripture with Holy Spirit then add your prayer link on the next page.

# Day 15

## Uproot

Father, root out every evil spirit from the hearts and minds of your people. Purify us for your glory, amen.

*"That he might present it to himself a glorious church, not having spot, or wrinkle, or any such thing; but that it should be holy and without blemish."*
*Ephesians 5:27*

🔖 Meditate on the scripture with Holy Spirit then add your prayer link on the next page.

# Day 16

### Removal

Father, remove all sinful fruit from my life. Prune me in the name of Jesus. (Uproot unforgiveness, abusive language, pride, lust, lewdness, bitterness, lying, etc.)

*"Every branch in Me that does not bear fruit, He takes away; and every branch that bears fruit, He prunes it so that it may bear more fruit." John 15:2*

 Meditate on the scripture with Holy Spirit then add your prayer link on the next page.

# Day 17

Preserve

Father, preserve and insulate me from personal and spiritual blows. Gird me in the armor of the Lord, amen.

*"Put on the whole armour of God, that ye may be able to stand against the wiles of the devil." Ephesians 6:11*

🔖 Meditate on the scripture with Holy Spirit then add your prayer link on the next page.

# Day 18

### Seal

Holy Spirit, seal me so that the enemy cannot open my mind or heart. Block any unauthorized transmissions from having access to my life and family, in Jesus name.

*"Now he which stablisheth us with you in Christ, and hath anointed us, is God; Who hath also sealed us, and given the earnest of the Spirit in our hearts." 2 Corinthians 1:21-22*

*"In whom ye also trusted, after that ye heard the word of truth, the gospel of your salvation: in whom also after that ye believed, ye were sealed with that holy Spirit of promise," Ephesians 1:13*

🖋 Meditate on the scripture with Holy Spirit then add your prayer link on the next page.

# Day 19

## Walk

Father, help me to walk in faith with soberness and all vigilance in the name of Jesus.

*"But without faith it is impossible to please him: for he that cometh to God must believe that he is, and that he is a rewarder of them that diligently seek him." Hebrews 11:6*

*"Be sober, be vigilant; because your adversary the devil, as a roaring lion, walketh about, seeking whom he may devour:" 1 Peter 5:8*

🕯 Meditate on the scripture with Holy Spirit then add your prayer link on the next page.

# Day 20

### Overflow

Father, help me to overflow in the joy of the Lord and in the hope of your goodness.

*"Then he said unto them, Go your way, eat the fat, and drink the sweet, and send portions unto them for whom nothing is prepared: forthis day is holy unto our Lord: neither be ye sorry; for the joy of the LORD is your strength." Nehemiah 8:10*

*"I had fainted, unless I had believed to see the goodness of the LORD in the land of the living." Psalm 27:13*

🖋 Meditate on the scripture with Holy Spirit then add your prayer link on the next page.

# Day 21

### Understanding

Holy Spirit, help me to understand your purpose in the world and in my life in Jesus name.

*"Howbeit when he, the Spirit of truth, is come, he will guide you into all truth: for he shall not speak of himself; but whatsoever he shall hear, that shall he speak: and he will shew you things to come."*

*John 16:13 "And when he is come, he will reprove the world of sin, and of righteousness, and of judgment." John 16:8*

🕊 Meditate on the scripture with Holy Spirit then add your prayer link on the next page.

## Day 22

### Newness

Father, I cry out for newness. Regenerate me in mind, body and soul. Cause me to prosper in the name of Jesus, amen.

*"Therefore if any man be in Christ, he is a new creature: old things are passed away; behold, all things are become new." 2 Corinthians 5:17*

*"Faithful is he that calleth you, who also will do it." Thessalonians 5:24*

*"Being confident of this very thing, that he which hath begun a good work in you will perform it until the day of Jesus Christ:" Philippians 1:6*

⚘ Meditate on the scripture with Holy Spirit then add your prayer link on the next page.

# Day 23

## Baptism

Father, baptize me with the fire of Holy Spirit. I desire the fullness of Holy Ghost in my life.

*"I indeed baptize you with water unto repentance: but he that cometh after me is mightier than I, whose shoes I am not worthy to bear: he shall baptize you with the Holy Ghost, and with fire:" Matthew 3:11*

Meditate on the scripture with Holy Spirit then add your prayer link on the next page.

# Day 24

## Mouth

Father, give me a mouth that will speak for you. Fill it with words of wisdom so that I can preach the good news of Christ to all men, amen.

*"For I will give you a mouth and wisdom, which all your adversaries shall not be able to gainsay nor resist." Luke 21:15*

🖋 Meditate on the scripture with Holy Spirit then add your prayer link on the next page.

# Day 25

### Cleanse

Father, cleanse me from ugly imaginations, in the name of Jesus.

*"Wash me throughly from mine iniquity, and cleanse me from my sin." Psalm 51:2*

*"Create in me a clean heart, O God; and renew a right spirit within me." Psalm 51:10*

✒ Meditate on the scripture with Holy Spirit then add your prayer link on the next page.

# Day 26

### Cry

Father, I cry out against the destruction of your people. I cry out for those who believe in false gods and false doctrines. Bring them to your fold.

*"The Lord is not slack concerning his promise, as some men count slackness; but is longsuffering to us-ward, not willing that any should perish, but that all should come to repentance." 2 Peter 3:9*

*And other sheep I have, which are not of this fold: them also I must bring, and they shall hear my voice; and there shall be one fold, and one shepherd." John 10:16*

🖎 Meditate on the scripture with Holy Spirit then add your prayer link on the next page.

# Day 27

### Interference

Father, I cry out against prophetic interference. Let the word of the Lord resound in the heavens and echo throughout the earth.

*"Wherein in time past ye walked according to the course of this world, according to the prince of the power of the air, the spirit that now worketh in the children of disobedience:" Ephesian 2:2*

🌿 Meditate on the scripture with Holy Spirit then add your prayer link on the next page.

# Day 28

## Condemn

Father, I condemn earthly, sensual and devilish wisdom. I condemn strife, evil works, envying and the like in my life. Put them to death in the name of Jesus.

*"But God hath chosen the foolish things of the world to confound the wise; and God hath chosen the weak things of the world to confound the things which are mighty;" 1 Corinthians 1:27*

*"For my thoughts are not your thoughts, neither are your ways my ways, saith the LORD." Isaiah 55:8*

*For the wisdom of this world is foolishness with God. For it is written, He taketh the wise in their own craftiness." 1 Corinthians 3:19*

*This wisdom descendeth not from above, but is earthly, sensual, devilish." James 3:15*

🖋 Meditate on the scripture with Holy Spirit then add your prayer link on the next page.

# Day 29

## Proof

Father, cause me to be a proof producer (one who bears spiritual fruit) in the name of Jesus. Cause men to see the evidence and begin to believe in you.

*"Believe me that I am in the Father, and the Father in me: or else believe me for the very works' sake." John 14:11*

*"But if I do, though ye believe not me, believe the works: that ye may know, and believe, that the Father is in me, and I in him." John 10:38*

Meditate on the scripture with Holy Spirit then add your prayer link on the next page.

# Day 30

Magnify

Father, magnify the Spirit of God within me.

*"And such as do wickedly against the covenant shall he corrupt by flatteries: but the people that do know their God shall be strong, and do exploits."* Daniel 11:32

*"Insomuch that they brought forth the sick into the streets, and laid them on beds and couches, that at the least the shadow of Peter passing by might overshadow some of them."* Acts 5:15

*"And God wrought special miracles by the hands of Paul: So that from his body were brought unto the sick handkerchiefs or aprons, and the diseases departed from them, and the evil spirits went out of them."* Acts 19:11-12

Meditate on the scripture with Holy Spirit then add your prayer link on the next page.

## Conclusion

*"And when he had taken the book, the four beasts and four and twenty elders fell down before the Lamb, having every one of them harps, and golden vials full of odours, which are the prayers of saints." Revelation 5:8*

According to Revelation 5:8, our prayers are odors that are placed in golden vials. They are stored and preserved as one would preserve jam or jellies. This signifies that our prayers are precious to God and are worthy of being gathered and kept so they are not spoiled. Since God places such a high value on our prayers, we should as well!

Prayers do not have to be long to have an eternal impact. They do not have to be laden with a multitude of words for God to hear them or his heart to respond to them. Therefore, let us continue to lift up our prayers to the Lord by faith, believing that he will respond with grace and favor toward us continually. Let us stand in confidence that all we ask in the name of Jesus will be done for us according to the good will and pleasure of the Father.

*"And whatsoever ye shall ask in my name, that will I do, that the Father may be glorified in the Son." John 14:13*

As we cover our families, homes, and selves let us remember to cover those we work with, sit beside in church, the state in which we live, and the nations of the world. Let us pray for righteous leaders to be in office. Let us use our mouths to call light into dark places where secret deals are struck. Where corruption lurks, where lies are fashioned, and where plots and schemes of the enemy are hatched.

*"For kings, and for all that are in authority; that we may lead a quiet and peaceable life in all godliness and honesty." 1 timothy 2:2*

Holy Spirit is not limited. He can gain access to any place in heaven, on earth or even below the earth. Therefore, let us pray with the spirit of wisdom securing

God's territory so that his kingdom can come and his will can be done on this earth as it is in heaven, amen (Matthew 6:10).

*"For he whom God hath sent speaketh the words of God: for God giveth not the Spirit by measure unto him." John 3:34*

www.ingramcontent.com/pod-product-compliance
Lightning Source LLC
Chambersburg PA
CBHW071410040426
42444CB00009B/2185